Cats

Written by Marilyn Woolley and Keith Pigdon
Photographs by Graham Meadows

Contents

1. Where do cats live?

Cats live all over the world. Some cats live with people. These cats are called pets. Pets are usually quite small.

Some cats live in the wild.
These cats can be very large,
like the tiger and the lion.
Some of these wild cats
also live in zoos.

2. What do cats look like?

All cats have whiskers,
pointed ears
and large eyes.
They have claws on their feet.

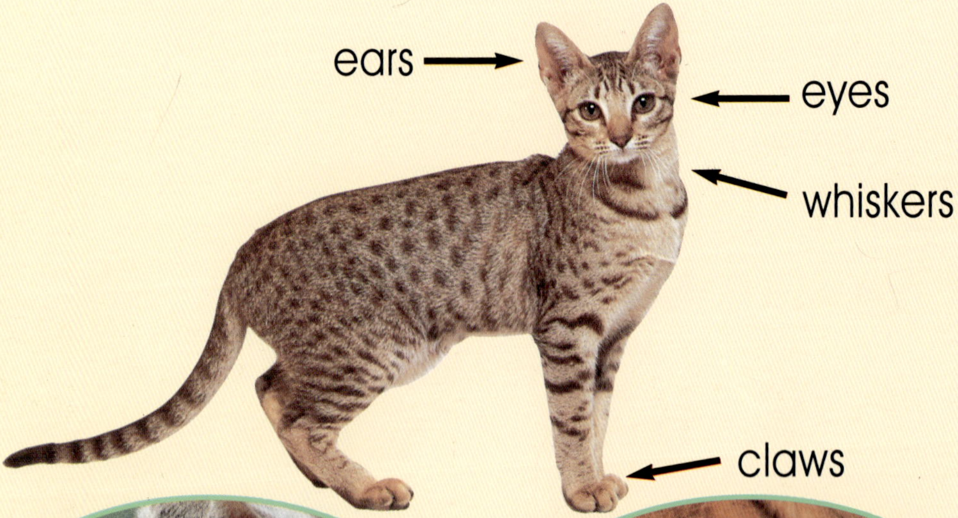

Cats have fur all over their bodies.
This fur can be short or long.
It can be many colours
and many patterns.
Cats use their rough tongues to lick,
clean and groom their fur.

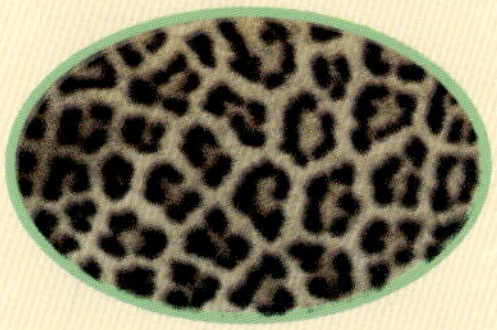

3. How do cats move?

Cats have special backbones that help them to run fast. They can arch their backs and stretch. They can jump, climb up and down and pounce on things.

Animals run in different ways.

Most cats can move very quickly. The cheetah is the fastest land animal on Earth.

4. What do cats do?

All cats
spend a lot of time
sleeping during the day.
Cats often begin
hunting after they
wake from a nap.
They hide in the long grass
or in trees and bushes.
Their spots and stripes
make them hard to see.

Cats like to play
and to sharpen their claws.
Pet cats chase balls,
mess up wool
and jump on shelves.

5. What do cats eat?

Cats eat meat.
They have very sharp teeth.
People raise cats to be tame,
but cats still like to hunt animals
smaller than themselves,
such as mice, rats, birds,
beetles and lizards.

6. How do cats care for their young?

Cats give birth to live young
and feed them on milk.
All young cats are born tiny,
blind and helpless.
The mother looks after them.
Sometimes she carries them
around in her mouth.
Young pet cats are called kittens.
Young wild cats are called cubs.

TO

SOPHIA,

LOVE FROM

....

Hi, I'm
SOPHIA!
What's your
name?

On a normal street like yours and mine,
It was a bright and sunny day.
Sophia saw, as she opened the door,
A gang of animals waiting to play.

The tiger loves taking centre stage,
He's quite the confident one.
But equally, and I'm sure you'll agree,
His shy friends are also fun.

Let'sss play,
SOPHIA!

Hide-and-seek's a favourite game,
It's Sophia versus giraffes.
Her careful disguise won't fool their eyes,
And it ends with smiles and laughs.

Here we come,
SOPHIA!

Some friends like to relax and snuggle,
Others creep about and are tickly.
The otters hug, the gorillas are snug,
And the porcupines are cute and prickly.

Wanna hug, SOPHIA?

The sloths love hanging out and snoozing,
While the monkeys swing about.
Sophia grins at the jumps and spins,
And the wild and cheeky shouts.

ZZZZZ

It's time to settle down for lunch,
Sophia's takes some beating.
Her friends have FRUITS,

GRASS, GRUBS and ROOTS,

There's an icky stench wafting
through the air,
And Sophia's turning greener!
It might just be, the hippo, you see,

Or perhaps the RING-TAILED LEMUR?!

Sophia spots the rhinos squabbling,
They're bickering and butting their heads.
She must put a stop, to their childish strop,
"I'll try a spot of juggling," she said.

Sophia's hair is a little bit messy,
"But my friends look much funnier!"
she thinks.

They're BUSHY and BRISTLY,
SPIKY and FRIZZY,
All coloured red, orange
and pinks.

Hooray! They've found a trampoline,
It's sure to raise a grin.

The giraffe takes flight,
And the hippo's a sight,
As they **LEAP** and

BOUNCE and **SPRING.**

Night night,
SOPHIA

Sophia is ready to head back home,
As night eclipses the day.
But there's still time,
For a little more rhyme,
As her friends have
SOMETHING TO
SAY....

She's fun!
She's clever!
She's friendly!
She's kind!
She really loves to play!

Sophia can't deny,
As she waves goodbye,

Sophia, now draw your different friends and tell us why they're so special.

Written by Joe Barnes
Illustrated by Cinzia Battistel
Designed by Alice Xavier

First published by HOMETOWN WORLD in 2019
Hometown World Ltd
1 Queen Street
Bath
BA1 1HE

Visit www.hometownworld.co.uk

Follow us @hometownworldbooks

ISBN 978-1-78979-135-8

Printed in Italy
HTW_PO201910

Hometown World